Ken Melvin

Pusserina
the
Wondercat

Written by Kenneth B. Melvin
Illustrated by Linda Albrecht

Acknowledgments

Inspiration: Bernice J.Melvin and R. Chris Martin

Ilustrations: The primary illustrator was the talented Linda Albrecht. A few illustrations were done by Ken Melvin and one by Thubakabra

Editorial Staff: Heather L. Boothe and Donna Alt-Bowes

Readers, Raters, and Listeners: Nick, Megan and Jacob Barger; Tommy Boothe; Kenny, Daphne, and Hannah Melvin; Sarah Jane Worley; Debbie and Spencer Alt; Deb Martin; Beverly Kissinger: Pat Potter; Martha Mullen; Cathy Banks; the Tidmore Vet staff; Dr. Doug Reynolds; Karen Banks; Julie O'Quinn; John; Aileen Englebert; Peggy Byars; Bud and Gail Gardner; Stan Brodsky; Ann and her Bookrack folks, Jim and Jean Tonjes; and Howard and Joan Bennett

Praise for
Pusserina the Wondercat

"This delightful collection of whimsical and eclectic poems, written by *Pusserina the Wondercat* and compiled by her servant Ken Melvin, is an enjoyable and educational read. All are told through the eyes, ears, and insights of yet another example of a feline marvel. The stunning illustrations by Linda Albrecht that accompany this amazing cat's stories are equally remarkable. If a cat were to write a poetry book, this would be, and is, it."

—Whit Gibbons, Ph.D.,
  Professor Emeritus of Ecology
  University of Georgia,
  author of *Snakes of the Southeast* and 19 other books

"*Pusserina the Wondercat* will delight the young and the young at heart. This book of charming poems and illustrations draws the reader into the slightly deranged world of the cat. Ken Melvin's elegant and whimsical poems reveal his deep understanding of animal behavior as well as his love of cats."

—William H. Gardner, Ph.D.,
  author of *Handling Truth*

"Ken Melvin has created a book of whimsy, charm, and love for the cat fancier. I was enchanted by insightful lines like, *Everywhere that Mary went,* the cat refused to go, as well as by poems that bring a big smile to my face, like one that begins, *Lots of kitties live in cities. Pusserina* has earned a treasured place on our bookshelves."

—Stanley L. Brodsky, Ph.D.,
  Clinical Psychologist

Pusserina the Wondercat
Written by Kenneth B. Melvin
Illustrated by Linda Albrecht

ISBN 978-1-63393-311-8

Published by

In association with

Preface

Despite being an avid student of animal behavior, and having been owned by numerous cats, I have never fully understood them. But recently, our new kitten, Pusserina, amazed me with her attempts to communicate. To my wonder, I began to understand the myriad nuances of "meow". Soon the puss regaled me with her cats-eye view of the world, stories of other cats, and flights of fancy. As she relates later, a genie had granted her wish to be a writer. But with this wish, there came a curse: She could only write in verse. Enough, let us visit with Pusserina and enter her world of felinity.

CAT

Who am I?
I am a big-eyed kitten,
Warm, and soft, and sweet
I am a lion in a jungle of small bushes.
I am a lap-cat.
A puss to snuggle and pat
I am meows, fangs, and fur
A claw, a purr, a paw
All of these,
And so much more

I'M A CAT

I'm a cat, not a bat
I am sleek, but not a rat
I often purr, and have nice fur
Sad to say, I have no hat
I like a pet, enjoy a pat
Came inside, sat on a mat
Someone said, "Who dat?"
I replied, "It's me, the cat."
Sometimes I wonder where it's at.

"What fun to be a cat!"
—CHRISTOPHER MORLEY

NOISES

It seems that everyone has their say,
It is nature's way
Mynah birds and parrots talk,
But the parrots also squawk
Donkeys bray, and horseys neigh,
But newts, they have no say
The mouse is meek, but it does squeak,
And sometimes makes a girl say, "Eek!"
Tigers growl, and wolves do howl
Coyotes wail, along the trail
And if you step right on its tail,
A pussycat will also wail
A rooster might crow, "cock-a-doodle-do",
While a kitten gives a mew
An owl cries, "who, who, who",
While the cow says "moo" to you
There's a sound I like to hear,
It is music to my ear
No, no, it's not "bow-wow",
But rather, the cat's meow

CAT MOVES

A nap on the lap, and then I wake
"Up puss, up," they say
"You can't stay, so go away."
I sit on the book, on the paper
"I can't read, with a cat on it,
Go away and write a sonnet."
"Off the stove, I've got to cook,
And don't give me that dirty look."
Just when I get in the groove,
It is always, move, move, move!
Ho, ho, ho, I just ate
A piece of meat right off your plate
Oh, oh, oh, here I go
Now once more, I'm on the floor.
I can't take it anymore
I'm telling you,
It's cat abuse!
I'll complain to Dr. Suess!

THE FINICKY CAT

With name brands, fill your cart
Don't give me that cheap stuff from Walmart
Don't cook my egg too long,
For me, a hard-boiled egg is wrong
I love Little Friskies,
Not those cheapo Kitty Wiskies
And I like Doritos--not Fritos
An apple, pear or berry,
Will not make me very merry
I'm a cat, not a fruit bat
If you cook a roast, take care,
You should know, I like mine rare
I am so finicky, so they say
No way!
I am a pussycat gourmet.

THREE LITTLE KITTENS

Three little kittens
They lost their mittens
They began to cry
Saddest kits I ever met
I say to them,
"Now don't you fret
Go out and play
We don't need mittens
Anyway."

THE GENIE

Many have asked, but few do know it,
How I became a pusscat poet
So listen all, to my story
In the woods, I made a foray
There I found a lamp of brass,
Hidden in the sassafras
A shiny thing, but very old,
Then I rubbed away the mold
From the lamp, smoke did swirl,
Wisps of it did curl and twirl,
And then I saw a fair young girl
She wore bangles, and dressed in silk,
I had never seen her ilk
On her face, she wore a frown,

Spotted me and looked around
"I see you, cat, you're the one.
You've rubbed me the wrong way.
I'm not supposed to wake today.
In fact, you woke me much too soon,
For you to get the usual boon,
No three wishes for you,
One wish will have to do.
It wasn't fair, it wasn't nice,
So you will have to pay the price.
And there is something worse,
With your wish, you get one curse.
But I'm a genie, not a meanie,
The curse will not be too bad,
It will not make you sad,
While the wish will make you glad,
So please, my cat, do not be mad."
I thought a while, then I did smile
"I wish to be a writer of renown,
To make my name and have some fame."
"I grant your wish, my cat,
A writer you shall be,
And that is that.
But with this gift, there comes the curse,
You can only write in verse."

SLEEP

A cat can sleep
In a bag, on a rag
In a box, on your socks
Snug as a bug, on your rug
She'll take a nap, on your lap
Then on the floor, she'll sleep some more
A cat can sleep
In a boat, on your coat
In the dirt, on your shirt
In the bed, on your head
On your hair, in the chair
Anywhere

"The small feline is a masterpiece."
—LEONARDO DA VINCI

LOST KITTEN

The kitten fell down the hole,
The space below was black as coal
Now she's on a cement floor
A sliver of light, marks a door
I hear them calling me
"Pusserina, where are you?"
What does a lost kitten do?
She gives a mew, a mew, a mew
Saved at last, warm and snug
Wrapped up in a loving hug

SPRING

The spring has sprung
The grass has riz
I wonder where the birdies is

ME

I must say, I am a pretty kitty
Smart I am, and often witty
I have a coat of many colors
There's some red upon my head
My nose is sort of pink, I think
My back fur is brown and russet
Watch out now, don't you muss it
It is slight, but I have an overbite
If you had fangs, you would too
I bite stuff, it's what I do
Take a look upon my chest,
A blaze of white marks my breast
I have stripes and am not spotty
I am just a kit cat hottie
My claws are black, my paws are white
All in all, I'm quite a sight.

"A home without a cat, and a well-fed, well-petted
and properly revered cat, may be a perfect home,
perhaps, but how can it prove its titles."
—MARK TWAIN

NEW HOME

My mommy was a calico
All her kittens loved her so
We curled up near her feet
Warm she was, tasty and sweet
With Sarah Jane and Hannah I would play
Until one day I went away
I moved in then, with Bernice and Ken
They had two cats, Princess and Xena,
They thought to call me Czarina
But I wound up named Pusserina
I was petted, got lots of love,
And fed until I got my fill
One lucky cat, I live there still

FAERIES

In the garden, come with me
Let us take a stroll
What wonders will we see?
Look, there is a big ol' troll
It is just part, of our garden art
Of stone and resin are they made
Here they rest, in sun and shade
Herons, coons, and there's a frog,
Two owls of stone, a turtle on a log
Cats dance while meercats stand erect

I count the fairies, there are five,
Late at night, they come alive
They sit under the bowers,
Peeking out among the flowers
Most dress in gowns of silk and laces
And they have such pretty faces
But Meg has a flower in her hair.
Otherwise, she is quite bare
Fiona is the largest, three-foot tall,
Cassandra has a crystal ball
Fawn flaps butterfly wings,
I love it when she sings
Fay is the tiny one, she is a hon
Some might think it is absurd,
That she rides a hummingbird

When the moon is full and bright,
The fae, they oft take flight
Despite the creatures of the night
Most of which do stay away
For if you make a fairy mad,
You will be so very sad
An owl was very rash one night,
It did try to bite a sprite
I never thought an owl could howl
Or perhaps it was a screech

Now it is the break of day,
Again, the fae come out to play
I hear Fawn sing, she's on the wing
Later, they will fade away
Most of them fly right by me
I'd love to be their friend,

But they don't sing to me
I'm just a cat, you see
Now they're perched up in a tree
The fairy folk, they love an oak

Near the garden, on a chair
I sit and watch them playing there
The fairy, Fay, the smallest one,
Lets her wings dry in the sun
Something brown is in the green today,
A sneaking rat is stalking Fay
I'm off the chair and on the rat
In the fight, I get a bite
Too much cat, away the rat
Now I sit and lick my wounds

The fae, they come to comfort me
I feel the soft touch of their wings
And then, to me, the fae, Fawn, sings
I know now, in all the world,
There is nothing sweeter than this,
As when you get a fairy's kiss

THE BALLAD OF KIT MCGEE

I knew a cat named Kit McGee
Who really loved to climb a tree
McGee was very, very, frisky
And what he did was very risky
He would prance, across a branch
And leap from limb to limb
McGee swung through the trees
With the greatest of ease
And the people passing by
Said, "Look, look, up in the sky.
It's amazing, see that cat.
He's a furry acrobat."

The birds would tweet and twit
They had thought the squirrels were nutty.
But there's one loony kit
When McGee came leaping by,
They would all take off and fly
With his jumps, and leaps, and twirls,
He managed to annoy the squirrels
That cat is mad as a hatter
They did chatter
To McGee, it did not matter

One day, McGee, he climbed so high
He could almost touch the sky
A flying squirrel came gliding by
McGee, he leaped upon it
Said he, "My, oh my, I can fly!"
But the weight was much too great.
And squirrel and cat soon met their fate
It was the end of Kit McGee
So all you kitties, listen to me
No matter how hard you try,
A pussycat just cannot fly

"CATS OFF THE TABLE!"

For the older cats,
The table was forbidden
But my folks were very smitten,
With this lovely little kitten
On the table I was set
And there I'd get a nice long pet
And, hey, I'm still there yet
So, to me, "Cats off the table!"
Is just another fable

PLAY WITH ME

Play with me
I'll be nice, you will see
No fangs for me
Roll the ball
And pull the string
A catnip mouse
Is just the thing
I'll jump up and grab your knee
Oops, sorry for the scratch on you
But, hey, it's what I do

CAT LADY

It takes a while, perhaps not yet
But you will get,
To look just like your pet
There was a lady from Phoenix City,
Who looked so much like her kitty
The lady's name was Rose,
And she had a pussycat nose
Her hair was blond, the cat's was tawny
Their eyes were blue
Both of them were well-groomed, too
As they sauntered to and fro,
People came to watch the show
They said, "There goes Rose, she is so pretty,
And that is one gorgeous kitty."
But others disagreed and said,
"She may be a catty cutie,
But she's not a beauty."
A person asked, "Why not?
I think she's very hot."
"Well, she may have a cute nose,
But I don't like her furry toes."

MARY

Mary had a little Persian
Of course she did, in this version
Its coat was white as snow
And everywhere that Mary went
The cat refused to go

MY RULES

Most kids are fun, to them I run
A few are fools, they need my rules
Don't cross me
Don't boss me
Don't toss me
For if you throw this kit,
You will get bit
The sharp things on my paws
Are claws
The sharp things in my jaws
Are fangs
Don't pull my tail, or I will wail
So don't be fools, heed my rules
Give them a try, or you will cry

MOO CAT

There once was a cat from Purdue
Who ate a steak, and burgers too
Then he would eat a roast
Have some chipped beef on toast
Instead of meowing, he'd moo.

HUMPTY DUMPTY

Humpty Dumpty sat on a wall
Humpty Dumpty had a great fall
All the king's horses and all the king's men
Could not put Humpty together again
Several cats came to the wall
They were sad to see the fall
"He was a good egg," they said,
"We are sorry he is dead
To his memory, we'll raise a cup,"
Then they shrugged, and lapped him up.

MY FEATHERED FRIENDS

I love birds, they don't like me
I'm a pussycat, you see
I'll just sit here, on this chair
There's a breeze, the day is fair
I'm so nice, and, oh so, sweet,
But all I hear is tweet, tweet, tweet!
A cat, a cat, a cat, they say,
Hoping I will go away
And way up in a tree,
A slim grey bird is mocking me
They hate kits, the little twits
Come on birdies, what's the matter
Please chill out and stop that chatter
I'm not scary, don't be wary
Just be calm and trust in me,
I'm not a bad guy, you will see
They say that many a feathered friend,
To birdy heaven, a cat did send
It wasn't me, I didn't do it
And if I did, I sure would rue it
So let us all just get along,
And so I'll listen to your song
I love to hear the birdies sing,
Little cat treats on the wing.

BAGS

I really hate a plastic bag,
All they do is crumple and sag
The paper ones will stand up tall,
And almost never fall
When on its side, a puss can hide
I know it is a pusscat quirk,
But in the bag I like to lurk
Now he's going to the store,
So Ken I nag,
Please get me a paper bag!

THE MINER

Way out west, lived Sam the miner
Who was, an absent-minded Forty-niner
In his house, he spilled gold dust,
Then he ranted and he cussed
He looked into a box of litter,
Then cried out, "It's kitty glitter"!

"A cat is nobody's fool."—HEYWOOD BROWN

THE GREAT CAT DRIVE OF '95

In the West, there was a rancher
They called him, Texas Ted
Of Ted, it was said
He was not quite right, in the head
But Ted was a man with a plan
"I will drive a herd of cats
From Austin to Kansas City,
And I will not lose a kitty."
When asked why,
He would reply
"It has never been done,
I will be the first one!"
Ted hired a motley crew
Five small cowboys on Shetland ponies,
And mini border collies, they were two
In just two days,
They rounded up all the strays
And so it began
The great cat drive of '95
Ted, 300 cats, and his crew
Five ponies, and two dogs, too

At first things went okay, few cats did stray
At a waterhole, the cats did lap
Then they stopped and took a nap,
Finally, Ted said "Move 'em out,
We're too slow, we've got to go
As they rode, the cowboys sang,
"Git along little kitty
You're on your way to Kansas City."

The wind was gusty, the trail was dusty
The kitties let out cries,
As the dust got in their eyes

A lone cowboy was passing by
When he hear their mournful cry
He stopped and stared in awe
A mighty herd of red-eyed cats
Swept up the draw
He turned away and rode the range
Thinking, this was awful strange.

Later on, they made their camp
While the cowboys lazed,
The little ponies grazed
It seems that they were off their feed,
And ate the local locoweed
Later on they would not work
And then the ponies went berserk
The cat herd was spooked
They ran and scattered, willy-nilly
While the dogs were driven silly
The dogs gave up and went to sleep
And in their dreams, they herded sheep

It was the end, my friend
Of the great cat drive of '95
And if you really think about it
The very idea of a cat herd
Is, of course
Quite absurd.

BAD CAT

Look outside, snow and rain
I'll stay inside, and be a pain
Aha, the stoves not hot
I'll jump on and bat a pot
There's some papers, shred 'em up
Oops, there goes another cup
Don't get in a stew,
It was not new
Do not be furious
I'm a cat, and cats are curious
"Go away." they say
"Scat, you cat!"
On the table, a plate of meat
Sneaking up, on little cat feet
Off I go, with the loot
'"Bad cat!" Now I get the boot
It's "Out you go!"
And here I am, in the snow

WHERE WE LIVE

Lots of kitties live in cities
Uptown cats live high on the hog,
Even better than the dog
Alley cats, they have it rough,
And they must be really tough
Their lives are gritty, in the city
Some cats live on the farm,
Often they stay in the barn
They work hard each day,
To keep the greedy mice away
Feral cats live in woods and alleys
There they eke out a living,
In a world that's unforgiving
Some kits live in towns, like me
I have a home, but still can roam
Run in the sun, sleep in the shade
Hey, hey, hey, I got it made.

CAT WASH

Oh no, a flea,
It's right on me
They fill the sink,
It's bad, I think
I make a run
Spencer says, "I caught her."
"Put her in the water."
Yowl and howl and do a flip
It's no use, I take a dip
I can't cope, with all this soap
On the counter, there I sat,
Looking like a drowned rat
But I'm happy, for says Ken
"I'll never wash this cat again."

"A purr vibrates the heart." —MARTHA MULLEN

DOWN BY THE LAKE

Let us stroll down by the lake
It's a walk I often take
There's a big heron on the bank,
A blue one with a pointed beak
It has been there for a week
It is still, as it does wait,
With a fish, it has a date
In the bright sun, the water shimmers,
Look, there are some water skimmers
Here's an osprey, watch it dive!
Splash! A fish wiggles in its beak
Now three turtles and a frog,
See them sunning on a log
Lots of things do catch my eye,
As I slowly saunter by

WONDER CAT

I am a hero in my dreams,
A supercat, it seems
I tie a cape around my nape,
Pull on my boots and sheathe my sword,
Put on a floppy, fancy hat
Dress to be the Wonder Cat
Now I'm quite a sight,
I am ready for fight and flight

In the sky I fly, up, up, and away,
To fight for truth, justice, and the pussycat way
Two kids in trouble, I get there on the double
Down, and down, and down I swoop,
Like a falcon in its stoop
Now two scared kids I see,
Beaten by a bad bully
They are brave, and they I save
The bad guy flees the scene,
For I have claws like Wolverine

Once more I'm on the go, I look below
And then, I lose my serenity

Some weasels mauling little kittens
Oh, the felinity!
A litter of kittens, there were five,
Only four are still alive
There's a kitten, getting bitten,

A weasel has her in its jaws.
Now I am here, out pop my claws
I am not nice to them,
In fact, I slice and dice 'em
The kittens watch, and mew and mew,
And soon there's naught but weasel stew

I cannot stay, I fly away
I see two tired swimmers in a pond
What shall I do? I hate the water
I do not have a magic wand
But I'm no dope, I find a rope
With my help, they both can cope
Later on, another villain do I seek,
It seems that he knows where I am weak
He pulls a giant water gun.
And soon he has me on the run
But I put an end to that,
Dropped a rock right on his hat

Later I go out to lunch
With Batman, Spidey, and the bunch
Oh, my gosh, what a crew!
I'm glad I'm a superhero too
Later, when I appear, the people cheer
One asks, "Who's that?
"It's Pusserina, the Wonder Cat."

TUXEDO CAT

For a tuxedo cat, black and white
Is normal
I like this cat, for he
Is very formal

FOOTBALL CATS

Look at names of football teams
Fierce critters abound, it seems
Lions and tigers and bears, oh my!
Elephants for the Crimson Tide
Panthers, wildcats, and cougars, too
Tigers at Auburn and LSU
I'm sad and mad,
It drives me bats
No teams are named
"The Pussycats"!

RESCUE CAT

In the shelter, cats await
Uncertain of their fate
In a cage, a kitten waits, bereft
So alone, the last one left
Now the lady comes to her
And leans into the cage
And feels a paw softly, softly, touch her face
She turns to her daughter, Sue
"It is written,
That I must have this kitten
I will call you Kittypat,
And I'll always love you
You shall be my rescue cat."

Five years later, to the day,
On the floor, the lady lay

"It's my heart, it hurts,
Kitty, Kitty, wake up Sue."
The kit wouldn't let her lady die
Raced down the hall, in full cry
In the room, she woke up Sue
Who called the fire-rescue crew
In the house, the cat still waits
Three weeks went by
Sue said, "She'll come home soon,
Kittypat, now don't you cry."
Here came the lady, through the door
Picks up the puss, off the floor
Feels the soft touch of her paw
"How I missed my little cat,
I'll always love you, Kittypat.
And you are, ever, my rescue cat."

THE CHAIR

On the chair,
A boy sat down
A screech and a claw,
And off he tore,
No sittin' on the kitten!

POET

I would bet,
You've never met
A cat like me
Not a cat like me
You might doubt me
And say
"Just a tabby cat is she,
That puss does not impress me."
So I say again
Just so you know it.
I am a furry feline poet

BOX

An empty box
Needs a puss
Some paper there,
For me to tear,
Let's make a fuss.

WORDS AND KIDS

A male cat is called a tom
A dam is a kitten's mom
Without a doe, a buck,
Is out of luck
On her, he does fawn
And livens up a frosty morn
In the sty, piglets are born
And now the sow, she is asleep
For she finds the male a boar
The baby heifer becomes a cow
And that's no bull
Then there are those who give us wool
A sheep girl is a ewe, to you
She may have a lamb,
If she hooks up with a ram
On the lakes, live ducks and drakes
A stallion and a mare
Make a cozy pair
In a shell, dwells the turtle
I wonder why, they are so fertile

PRINCESS

Princess is a Siamese
She's a puss I like to tease
Slowly I creep,
While she is asleep
I pounce with a yowl
She gives out a howl
Lots of fun
See her run!

TAILS

Cats wave their tails,
When they are mad,
And purr when they are happy
I think dogs are kind of sappy
They wave their tails,
When they are happy

"A kitten is in the animal world what a rosebud is in the garden."
—ROBERT SOUTHEY

BAD DOG

A dog came in my yard today
Not too big, and sort of black
Looked at Ken and gave a growl
I did fluff and arch my back
Telling Ken I got his back
As I charged I gave a yowl,
Here I came, hissin' and spittin',
The dog saw one fearsome kitten
And so he beat a fast retreat
A dog came in the yard today
Tucked in his tail and ran away

"There's no need for a piece of sculpture in a home that has a cat."
—WESLEY BATES

THE PERFECT CAT

It could be a he, more likely a she
Probably a female, rather than a he-male
But I could be wrong
A tom could sing your song
She walks so stately, sits sedately
Sweetest cat you'll ever meet
She is sleek, but not too meek
The kit is gutsy, not too nutsy
The perfect cat
She is brave, loyal and true
And very, very, fond of you
In her paws, she has sharp claws
Not too thin and not too fat
The perfect cat
You may disagree with me
You may have a different notion
For each puss has her own love potion
But you must remember
It is you she'll mesmerize
With her lovely, deep green eyes
It is amazing, don't you see
The perfect cat
Sounds just like me!

AT THE ZOO

In the zoo, a little kit
By the cages, he did sit
"Hi, big cats, what do you say?"
"I am tiger, hear me growl!"
The little puss began to yowl
"You're too loud, stop the howl."
"I am lion, hear me roar!"
"Please, not now, my ears are sore."
The cat was sad, he walked away
"They could not purr", I heard him say

"God made the cat so that man could have
the pleasure of caressing a tiger."—VICTOR HUGO

CAT KILLS

Over a year, it is said
Cats kill a billion birds
We take our toll of mouse and mole,
We are not nice, to rats and mice
We get the blame, and a bad name
But please stop the invective,
And look at this, from my perspective
If there were no hungry cats
Your cities would teem with rats,
And the busy hordes of moles,
Would fill your lawn just full of holes
Having piles of mice up to your posterior,
Would certainly lead to mass hysteria
And think if all those birdies bred
Flocks of birds will fill the skies
Bird poop would rain upon your head
Feathers would get in your eyes
I want you to think about that
Then go out and thank a cat.

NICE CATS

In days of old,
When cats were bold
They kept the houses,
Free of mouses
Today the cats are very nice
Into your house they bring the mice.

THE PAPER

Reading the paper
Here I come
Rip and shred
"Stop it", he said,
But pats my head

"A mouse in the paw
is worth two in the bush."
—PUSSERINA

LESSONS LEARNED

Some things you just have to learn,
I saw a movement in the fern
A slender lizard, kind of blue
I pounced right on its back
And then I had a lizard snack
Later, I came in the door,
And then I fell right on the floor
Got up again, again I fell
In a while, I tried to jump
Again I fell, right on my rump
Now Ken picks up his pet,
And off we go, to the vet
He says, "She ate a blue-tailed skink, I think.
And now she's one sick cat."
Hey, I knew that
It takes a week for me to heal
Finally, better I do feel
Another lesson learned
Now the lizards will be spurned

TABBY CATS

Leopards, cheetahs, and ocelots,
Are the cats with lots of spots
While pumas are quite plain,
As are the lions, but for their mane
Of the rest, just two types,
Come equipped with stripes
One's the tiger, feared by all
The other is one you'd rather meet,
The little tabby, oh so sweet

PRETTY

I'm so pretty
I'm a kitty
My eyes are green
My coat's got sheen
I have big paws
With lots of claws
I'm a beaut
And very cute
I'm so buff
With lots of fluff
And that's enough

CAT DANCING

I once knew a cat from Winokee
Of course, she was a furry Okie
Her name was Lola,
She was a dancer
While other cats might like to sing,
For Lola, dancing was her thing
In a barn dance, she had a fling

Any partner would do
She did not care
Danced with a pig, a cat and a hare
Found a fox, he was hot
Of course, they did a foxtrot
Then she danced a jig with a pig
Met a tomcat, who she kissed
They went out and did the twist
And then, as was her habit
She danced with a big white rabbit
As the band began to bop,
They pranced and danced the bunny hop
The last dance was a Cha Cha
Her partner said, "My name is Mr. Ed,
I am a horse, of course."
Two days passed, and then
Lola went out again
She found a bar with karaoke,
Perfect for a dancing Okie
Found a tom with lots of pep
Perfect for a Texas two-step
With a hepcat, cut a rug
As they did the jitterbug
Took a break and ate a mango
Then she glided in a tango
Lola was known all over town
As a dancer of renown
She dropped into a Polish bar
Where the band cried, "Lola"
And then they played the "Too Cat Polka"
As they sang the song
The crowd sung along
"She's too cat, much too cat
Much too cat for me, Hey"

Later on, she took the floor
The crowd began to shout,
"That's what it's all about!"
As the dancing furry Okie,
Went and did the hokey-pokey

SAD POEM

Way back,
In the yard
Lie the cats of yesteryear
Shed a tear
For Zorro, Sundance and Caprice
Raven, Xena, the Grey Bomb,
Princess and of course, old Tom,
In the yard still they lie.
When you pass by, give a sigh.
Sleeping 'neath the sod
When you pass, give a nod.

DAWN

Early in the morning,
The puss greets the dawn
With a great big yawn.

CHASE

Two big dogs
Came in my space
It is me they choose to chase
I'm so fast
Ran up a tree
They can't catch me
Woof, woof, so they bark
But I'm safe on the bark

BILL

On the couch,
Bill's asleep
Up his leg
I do creep
On his tummy
It's so yummy
What a comfy spot
I really like it
a lot
Not too cold, and not too hot
A perfect fit
For a sleepy kit

MEGAN

Ken's gone away, alone today
Now here comes Heather's daughter, Megan
I think she thinks that cat food stinks,
Perhaps she is a vegan
Sweetest girl you'd ever meet,
She'll get me some food to eat
Even though she has an allergy.
Megan's very nice to me
Uh, oh, I see her start to sweat,
Now I'll never get a pet
She's too near, she starts to tear,
Oh, no, she's turning red
I don't know if I'll get fed
Please, dear Megan, don't throw up,
Go away and pet a pup!

ZORRO

Ken had a cat named Zorro
A brave puss was he,
He went to the lake
And fought a big snake,
A big black one
The large snake won
A fang in the paw,
Will make it real sore
They rushed to the vet
And Ken saved his pet
So:
If you go to the lake
Watch out for the snake

TOMMY

I love a boy named Tommy
It's said he looks like me
'Cause the fur on his head
Is a nice bright red
A handsome lad is he

NAP

Don't need a map
To take a nap
Just sit down,
I'm on your lap

BUGS

Flit, flit, flit
I jump and twirl,
And catch it,
On the run,
Bugs are fun!

IN THE GARDEN

In the garden
The flowers bloom
For a puss
There's lots of room
There I roam
It is my home.
Sometimes we find holes
And in the holes reside the moles,
Birds and bugs, and lizards too
Oh, what's a busy puss to do
Sometimes a butterfly,
Hard to catch, although I try
It's paradise
But don't pounce on a bug that buzzes.
Heed my advice
Because I'm nice
Hear it from me
Never, never bite a bee!

ICE

I go out
There's cold and ice
Not so nice
Don't have to worry
When you're all furry

GRITS

Don't like grits
They're not for kits
Won't eat a beet,
But I like meat
Don't like jam,
A cat I am.
Give me some ham

RUG

On the rug
Here I lie
Watch your step
And walk on by
I tread on thee
Don't tread on me

CAT PREEN

Lick my paw,
Wash my face
Groom and preen,
Til I'm clean
And I'm pretty and so neat,
Right down to my furry feet

CHAIR

Clawed on a chair
They yelled at me
"Bad cat"!
I'll go out
And scratch a tree.

PRINCESS PUSS

Princess is a Siamese
If you please
She's a real beauty,
But very snooty
Walks on by
Her tail held high
Not too smitten,
With this kitten
I want to play
"No, not today"

HERMY

Hermy's a puss,
Kind of a wuss
One ear is torn,
He looks forlorn
The little guy,
Is very shy,
Just let him lie
He's sad today,
So go away
Tomorrow is
Another day

SQUIRRELS

Big grey squirrels stay in the yard
Catching them is very hard
As soon as they see me
Like a flash, they're up a tree
The little squirrels stay on the ground
Stupid they are, and often brown
Not too smart, and kind of slow
Crawl around and stay so low
But I can catch them
This I know

HARRY

I know a puss named Harry
He's big and fat
A really swell cat
A very nice fellow
We call him "mellow yellow"

MOLE

Brought my Ken a gift today,
A very tasty mole
I laid it on the rug
But all he said was,
"Ugh".

THE LAWN

Working on the lawn today
Ken mows and rakes
I keep the moles at bay
A passing lady stops to say,
"What a pretty cat"
Oh yes, she made my day!

FANCY FEAST

Fancy Feast's my favorite food
Puts me in a real good mood
Like my 'Lil Friskies too
Of course a runny egg will do
Then I'll share a mouse with you

KEN

I own a guy named Ken
He pets me now and then,
And often strokes my fur,
And all I have to do
Is purr

SNOW

A while ago,
Ken took me out into the snow
"Play", he said
But it was cold
And it was wet
No, no, not this pet
Into the house ran I
Snow falling from the sky
It's worse than rain
And for this puss, rain's a pain.

TAIL

A big grey male
He bit my tail
Ken yelled "Bad Cat"
And off he went
But my tail was sort of bent
It's sad to be a little cat
With a tail just like a rat
Waited for my fur to grow
It did, but oh so very slow

XENA

Xena was black
Her eyes were green,
Hissed and spit
She was mean
And I was just a 'lil kit

RON

Ron's a cat I know
He's always on the go
He scampers all about
But you better watch out
He'll nibble on your toe

PUSS AND BOOTS

A movie "Puss and Boots" was on TV
That dashing cat is right for me
He was so fine
He's on my mind
A handsome puss is he

CARS

The cars rush on by
They do not stop to cry,
For the creatures on the road
The squirrel, he ran around
The car caught him on the bound
There was a splat
And now he's flat
Here is where an armadillo fell.
The victim of a truck
Looks like a possum on half-shell
Slow, and out of luck.
So all you cats, beware
And take care

LOST ONES

I lost my mom,
And Xena too
Where did they go?
I do not know.
A cat can cry.

THE GIFT

Christmas is hither,
And still I dither
What then, can I give my Ken?
The moles are in their holes.
The birds are on the wing.
Nary a mouse, is near the house
Can't think of anything
Oh, I know what I'll do
I'll give him a warm cat rub
Lots of fur, and a loud purr

FERAL CATS

In the wild, some cats survive
By their wits, they stay alive
These feral cats must always roam,
For they lack a loving home
They never get a pet,
Or see a vet
I wonder how they came to be
Are they lost?
Were they tossed?
It worries me.

EASTER

Easter morn, the day is sunny
Where is the Easter bunny?
He brings us eggs and candy
I think he is rather dandy
But is it fair, for a hare,
To get all the credit there?
What about the Easter chicken?
Bunnies are cute, but kitties are pretty
Why not the Easter kitty?

Now the Easter eggs are hid,
Just enough to fool a kid
In the sofa, under the rug,
On the table, in the chair
Behind the door, on the floor
I'll sneak a peek
Only one egg do I seek
Now the kids are on the run
Oh boy, this is fun
Oops, I hear a crunch
There's an egg that's not for lunch

For a while, I'm in a bind
Not one egg, do I find
Oh, here's one, it's big and blue
There, there, under the chair!
I roll it out, my day is spoiled
For you see, it is hard-boiled

SNAKE

In the garden, I did lay
It was early in the day
I saw the grass begin to sway
Snake! It's small and kind of grey
Slowly it did slither,
I was thinking, snake come hither
Stalking slow, paw by paw
Pounced! The snake hung from my jaw
Out of the brush I pranced
My tail held high
In my garden I have no fear
My rule is:
No snakes here!

MUFFY

There once was a pussycat named Muffy
She was oh so very fluffy
She sat on a chair
And shed lots of hair
Now her folks are all huffy.

THE TREE

In the early Christmas morn,
Not a creature was stirring
Except for the cats
We sat in awe
What a tree!
Did we see
A star at the top, tinsel so shiny
Painted eggs, and reindeer so tiny
I had to give a ball a bat
While Xena pulled the tinsel down
Princess pounced, and that was that
The paper in the bags,
Soon became a pile of rags
Candy canes flew out the door
Now I hear another sound
Our folks are getting up
It was fun, I've got to run
The other cats play on the floor
Not me,
I'm out the door.

LOVE

As many folks have learned,
A cat's love must be earned
Feed me, pet me, don't upset me
You must please me, never tease me
Gaze deep into my emerald eyes,
And know I do not tell you lies
And know, how strong are our ties
Softly I lay my paw,
On your hand
Just so you understand
It is you that I adore
I lie now on your chest
I purr and tread
You stroke my head
You pet my toes
I lick your nose
We are one.

"The cat. He walked by himself, and all places were alike to him."
—RUDYARD KIPLING

CAT AND SEAL

There once was a cat from Mobile
Who loved a sleek young seal
They married, of course
Rode away on a horse
To me,
This seems rather unreal.

MARTHA'S CAT

There once was a kitty named Sue
Who didn't know what to do
She lived in a house
With three cats and a mouse,
Two dogs, a hamster and a fish,
A parrot and a cock-a-too
'Every day, she did pray,
"Oh Lord, let me out of this zoo!"

KITTEN ON THE KEYS

A kitten on the keys,
She is all around, up and down
Click, click, click
Heard a shout
Watch the paper flying out.
Got to run,
But it was fun.

DING DONG BELL

The cat fell in the well
He heard a sound,
And looked around
He saw a boy
"I'm Timmy, I'll help you," he said.
You can sit on my head.
Do not fret, they'll save us yet."
Then along came Lassie.
All the way from Tallahassee
The dog went bark, bark, bark
The boy did holler
Meow, meow, meow, cried the puss
They made a great big fuss
And soon were saved
The cat said, "I owe you this."
And gave the dog a great big kiss

IZZY

There once was a kitten named Izzy
Who was often in a tizzy
Every day, without fail
He would chase his tail
Until he got rather dizzy

"Don't eat cheap cat food. Make them
give you the good stuff!"—PUSSERINA

TRUE GRIT

They say
It is better to give than to receive
I agree
You can have my allergy
Once in a while, I get the grit
It is tough, my skin gets rough
I groom and gnaw,
'Til I am raw
It will not go away
I get the comb and then the brush
From my head, down to my tush
It will not go away
Now I know what's coming next
I know I will be sorely vexed
Off we go, to the vet
A poke, a prod, I get a shot
Fun it's not
But in a week, I'm nice and sleek
You would call me pretty,
Or at least say,
"No more gritty kitty"

WATER

It is spring, we cats are out
On the patio, we lie about
In the warm sun we drowse
We are sleepy, no meows
Oh no, here comes the water!
Now the cats are getting wet
That's no way to treat a pet
No way to please, a Siamese
A tabby cat, has no rain hat
Turn it off, be a buddy
Look, the garden's getting muddy
Water's fine, in the dish
But remember, we're not fish!

SPIDERS

Spiders, it seems, are everywhere
In the garden, on the chair
In their web they wait,
For a bug to meet its fate
Most of them just crawl and creep
But some of them will take a leap
On their web, the spiders surf
Do not invade their turf
Leave them alone, pass on by
I will tell you why
Do not pounce, don't be hasty
First of all, they are not tasty
The big ones will bite
Stay off of their site
And out of their sight
Itsy bitsy ones are easy prey
But not an ounce, do they weigh
Not worth a pounce, I say
They have icky sticky feet
And are not even good to eat

SNAKES

Don't like snakes
They hiss and bite
Close to the soil they coil
In the grass, they're hard to see
If they're big, a cat should flee
If they rattle, don't do battle
If still they lie, just pass on by
Never, never, wake a snake
But small ones are okay by me
For they are just prey for me
They are not scary, but quite wary
They slither, hither and yon,
Until they get pounced upon
Alas, there is no pardon
For a snake,
In my garden

PAT

There once was a lady named Pat
Who owned a nasty cat
The bad cat bit her
Right on her sitter,
And she traded it in for a rat.

MARIE

There once was a puss from Paree
Who went by the name of Marie
Cats did pursue her
And often did woo her
They tested her mettle
But she would not settle
For just any Tom, Dick or Harry

THE HUNT

I'm outside, in hunting mode
First of all, I see a toad
It is not for me today
So toad, please go away
Some butterflies come flitting by
Fun, but not worth a try
Here's a buzzing bug, a bee
I have learned to let it be
Hey, hey, hey, there's a jay
Now my walk becomes a stalk
That blue jay will be my prey
But somehow I caught its eye
And away the jay does fly

Some big brown birds, kind of rash
For in the leaves they thrash
Slow and low I creep
Two of them, I have my pick
But, alas, they are too quick

Later, I wait, by a hole
And from the hole, out pops a mole
A tasty mole does make my day
And, as they say
A mole in the paw is better
Than two birds in the brush

RENE', THE PUSSYCAT GOURMET

There was a prissy puss from New York
Who ate with a knife and a fork
He was so polite
He did everything right
He'd say, "Please pass the pork."
When served wine he'd sniff the cork
But Rene', he would say
I'd much prefer a café au lait
He was so sedate
His manners were great
The waiters watched in awe,
As he ate without a flaw

Rene' was a hoot, he loved to laugh
On being served the rabbit stew
Said he, "Waiter, come here, please do,
There is a hare in my stew."
When he ordered lobster or rabbit,
He'd tie a bib around his neck
But Rene' had one bad habit,
For when presented with the check
Rene' would leap right on the floor,
And then he took off out the door

René

CAT HATERS OF NOTE

It seems that many dictators
Can be counted as cat haters
There was a warlord, Genghis Kahn
He set 1000 cats alight
Used them to win a fight
Used them to burn a city
For cats and man, he had no pity
Remy, of the Inquisition,
Cats were demons, he declared
He was a man with a mission
Burn the witches and their cats
Then there was Hitler, the top Nazi
Did not like a little katze
And I would not give a Frito,
For a tyrant named Benito
I'm not sure of Mao Tse Tung
We cats called him, Mousie Dung
Napoleon, Emperor of France
So scared of cats, he wet his pants
Saw a cat, he could not hack it
Put his hand inside his jacket
These evil men have passed away
But I know where they are today
In the depths of hell, they dwell
Among the demon cats of hell
Cats who love to hear the haters squawk
When they stick them with a fork

HALLOWEEN

Halloween is not my favorite scene,
To a cat, some folks are mean
But then again, it can be fun
And now, with the waning of the light,
I see some kids, they're quite a sight
Here they come down my street
I hear them saying "Trick or treat"
Oh my gosh, there is a troll,
Watch him eat a tootsie roll
The little witches count their riches,
Then they go and get some more
Now my kids are at the door
Here's a mummy, with his mommy

Now I look and see my Tommy
Wow!
He's a scary little zombie
There's a wolf, it's kind of were
Oh me, I think he's coming here,
Big bad fangs, and lots of hair
Here's an ogre, I think it's Shrek
And a monster, bolt in neck,
Orcs, and rats and cats and bats
Okay, that's enough for me
Other cats go outside and hide,
Not for me, I stay inside.

BEARS

Bears live in the woods
Sometimes nature is a giver
Salmon come to them
In the river

I live in a house
With a man
Salmon come to me
In a can

THE WITCH'S CAT

In days of yore, near the shore
There was a town called Westwich
It had ten shops, a forge, a church
A stable, and the Wayward Inn
The little town, it was not rich
It had one doctor, a preacher and a witch
Wanda had a little shop
She sold herbs, charms and notions,
And, in the back, a few love potions

Some said she was a witch
And called her "Wicked Wanda'"
For she had a pointy hat,
And, of course, a big black cat
Her hair was red, a lady fair
Who oft wore flowers in her hair
And to most folks, she seemed nice
But sometimes, in the dark of night,
When the moon was not too bright
A witch-like figure flew
Was it someone we all knew?

Then a new preacher came to town
An angry man who wore a frown
He was squat and stout
And his eyes bulged out
But his voice was very loud
And soon he drew a crowd
He did rant and he did rave,
About the many souls he'd save
"The Wayward Inn is full of sin."
He did shout
"And I'm the man to root it out!"

Later on, the preacher man
Walked into Wanda's shop
"Here, there is a witch I smell'
And her big black cat from Hell!"
"Listen to what I say,
the wages of sin, will not pay!"
He kicked her cat, and walked away

Her eyes blazed red
And then she said,
"My good cat, he'll pay for that
Frogs I need, and frogs you'll get
Lots of frogs, I know you can
Out the door, the big cat ran
Out the door, and to the moor
For the bogs, were full of frogs
And soon her shop was full of frogs
Green and brown, and some with spots
They all went in the witch's pots
"Cauldron burn and cauldron bubble,
Someone's in a lot of trouble."
In the pots went bats and newts
Lizard's gizzards, in she threw,
As she stirred the stinking stew
A real old-fashioned witch's brew
"It's been a long time since I cast a spell,
I'm not sure it will work out well."
As she chanted, the puss did purr
He had a lot of faith in her

Meanwhile, in the small town square
The preacher man began to rant
But only ten townsfolk were there
"The witch, and her devil cat,
Must burn, I'll see to that."
Then he choked, his face turned green
Several townsfolk fled the scene
He was distraught, and then he thought
My speech is gone, I must ad-lib it
He strained a bit, and then croaked out,
"Ribbit, ribbit, ribbit"

DUCKS

Nearby there's a little pond
Of which, I am very fond
In the pond, there are some ducks
Their heads are mainly green,
And their down is kind of brown
Across the pond they paddle,
But on the bank they waddle
Fun to watch, but hard to catch
I won't wade through all that muck,
Just to catch a silly duck
Across the pond the ducklings go,
Mom has them all in a row
A duck swims near the shore
Kind of silly, black and white
I think it's kind of daft
Or maybe Daffy
I edge out on a little raft
Uh, oh, the goose is loose
And here it comes
A big white honky thing
Its beak is snapping, wings a flapping
Oh no, the goose is after me
Now I run up a nearby tree
Watching ducks has been fun.
But now it's time to run

BAD NAMES

Critters unite, it is insane
How folks take our names in vain
They use them fast and loose,
There's a filthy pig, a silly goose
She is catty, an old bat
He's a cur, but has no fur
Some are timid as a mouse,
Others just a dirty louse

He's a wolf, she's a cougar
Both do prey, they say
A dimwit is a silly ass
A sneak, a snake in the grass
A weasel is another sneak
A skunk does have a certain reek

Don't pig out and be a hog
They call a girl a female dog
Why not say she is a witch?
They often say, "you dirty dog", "you dirty rat."
One thing makes me glad, and that is that,
They never say, "You dirty cat."

RHONDA'S FIT

There once was a lady named Rhonda,
Who owned a tiny Honda
It was a tight Fit,
For her and her kit
As they went hither and yonder
She wanted to tour the USA
But thought, I can't go all the way
What shall I do? It came to her,
When she heard her cat, Matt, start to purr
Rhonda gave the puss driving lessons
Matt learned to drive in just six sessions
The town was not his scene,
Because he could not tell red from green
But the puss did great,
When cruising down the interstate
First they drove to Madison,
And stayed at the Radisson
Then down I-50, the cat did drive
Kept the Fit at seventy-five
First they stopped at Tuscaloosa,
And ate some tasty barbeque
Later on, they took I-10

All the way to New Orleans,
Where they dined on rice and beans
Came back again, on I-10

Later visited Gulf Shores
Where they took some tours
There seemed to be so much to do
Saw some pirates, dolphins, and a zoo
The East on I-10 again
In Florida, they took the pike
A road that Matt did like
Finally, they got to Disney
Where they met a real big mouse,
And got to tour a haunted house
Coming back, they stopped at Pensacola
For some shrimp and Coca-Cola
Stayed in Tuscaloosa,
By the river, in an inn
They left just in the Nick of time,
For the Tide was coming in

Near to home they made a stop
Later on they met a cop
He looked inside the Fit
Behind the wheel, there was a kit

"Madam, there's a cat, a cat, do you know that?"
"Of course I do, his name is Matt.
He just got his license today."
"Okay, be on your way."
And then he walked away,
Thinking, that makes sense,
I guess--or does it?
As they drove away,
Rhonda said, "Well my, pet,
It was a very good thing.
That we stopped at the vet."

ODE TO A TOAD

Here comes a toad
Across the road
Hop, hop, hop
It has a ways to go,
But it is very slow
Oh, oh, oh
Now the toad is flat and gnarly
Got run over by a Harley
In the garden, there's another
Maybe it's his brother

Here it sits, squat and dumpy
Mr. Toad, your skin is lumpy
In fact, it's rather bumpy
Mr. Toad, you are no cutie
Next to you, a frog's a beauty
Your belly is rather pasty,
You are not at all tasty
For a meal, you will not do
Mr. Toad, what good are you?
I would never eat a toad
Even a toad, alamode

SIS

My sister's name was Daisy,
A perky kitten, kind of crazy
A little fluffy kit cat cutie
Folks would say, "Oh, what a beauty!"
I must agree, for you see,
Daisy looks a lot like me.

"Cat: A fang, a paw, a purr, a claw—
and so much more"—KEN MELVIN

LITTLE GIRLS

Among my loves, are little girls
Lovely kids, with lots of curls
Like the boys, they bring cat toys
They don't play rough,
They are real sweet
The best little girls you'd ever meet
The little girls are oh, so, nice
But sad to say, they have one vice
For sometimes, they run amok
Then this kitty's out of luck
An open bag, in which I nose
Uh, oh, it's full of clothes
"Let's dress up the puss," they say
Oh no, I cannot get away
My head has red fur on it
I don't need a silly bonnet
Hey, my name's not Molly,
I am not a dolly
Unlike the three little kittens,
I will never miss these mittens
I don't mind the pretty scarf,
But this dress will make me barf
Come on girls, don't dress me up,
Go away and dress a pup

GROUPS

All groups of critters have a name,
I know not, from whence they came
Some are tame, and some are lame
There are cow herds, and flocks of birds,
Packs and prides and hives and tribes
For fish, schools and shoals are all the same
The sheep often form a flock
Here we see the ewes and rams,
Lots of dams, and little lambs
Some names really fit, from where I sit
A glint of goldfish, a peep of chicks,
A pack of dogs, a passel of hogs
Other names seem rather strange
I've never seen a salmon run,
But it would be a lot of fun
That several whales fit in a pod,
Seems to me, to be rather odd
Why are there wisdoms of wombats?
They are not as smart as cats
Why not owls, the sagest birds?
In the sea, it is said,
Clams and oysters go to bed
Lots of ants will form an army,

While other bugs are merely swarmy
In the hives of bees,
Live workers, drones, and a queen
For the bees have monarchies
But the solo bees are humble,
In the flowers they do bumble
And I should need some diapers,
If I should see a den of vipers
Baboons and boy scouts in a group,

Strange to say, are called a troop
In the sea, as a rule,
Is where the smart fish go to school
But, despite the rumors,
We never see a pack of pumas
As most cats live alone
A herd of cats, I can't condone
But it is my perception,
That there is one exception
The lion is a kingly beast,
On other critters does he feast
He has a silky mane, a tawny hide,
And of course, he has his pride

CAT FIGHTS

As a kitten, I was bitten,
As a cat, an end to that
Later then, I won out,
And oft put Xena to rout
Princess would not fight,
She would rather leave the site
At times, a yell would end the fight,
A splash of water would
Make us see the light
"Out you go," was the cry
We got the boot
We said bye, bye
We two cats were on our way,
We'll fight again another day.

EATING

Eating's something we all do
For great white sharks,
A seal's a treat
As well as me and you
The horse, he dotes on oats
The bear thinks fish,
Are quite a dish
Some folks love beans and rice
I think mice are nice,
And will suffice.

THE DOOR

Sitting on the stoop
Waiting
The door opens
"In or out," he says
"Make up your mind."
Hmm, let's see
What will I do
Don't rush me
I'll think about it
Don't have a fit,
It will only take a bit
Sitting on the stoop
Waiting

OWLS

When the moon is on the wane,
The owls take wing
In the night they reign
In the dark, they do their thing
Who, who, who,
Where are you?
Their beaks are sharp and hooked,
They have their eyes up front
And now they're on the hunt
Since they all eat meat,
A pussycat is quite a treat
So in the night, if you do prowl
Beware, beware, of the great horned owl
I think the pigmy owls are cute
Otherwise
I don't give a hoot

PUSSYCAT NATION

There is lots of variation,
Across the pussycat nation
Angoras have long hair,
While the Sphinx is almost bare
The bobcats have been robbed,
For their tails are bobbed
I give thanks,
I'm not a Manx
No tails have they,
No tails at all
Siamese tails have a crick,
While Persian tails are rather thick
The Siamese seem very tall,
Because their ears are quite erect
Tabbies take the middle road
Because, of course, we are purr-fect

BYE, BYE

It was a festive holiday,
And now the people go away
See you and bye, bye, they say
And now we are alone today
There they go, out the door,
I wish that they could stay some more
I'm sure they will come back again
Until then, I'll sit on Ken

ZOMBIE CATS

I had a scary dream last night
It gave me an awful fright
There the day was dark and dreary,
The place I was, was very eerie
Here sat a raven in an oak,
It gave a croak, a croak, a croak
Something wicked this way comes
And then the zombie cats I see,
Oh my gosh, they number three
So I try to climb a tree
Up I go, the bark gives way
It is not my day
My leg is hurt, and now I know,
I cannot run, I'm much too slow

Down the road, I see a church
Here they come, they limp and lurch,
On broken claws and mangled paws
Now I see a cat and her kits,
I give her a howl, then a yowl
They run and hide away
They will be safe, at least today,
For I lead three cats astray

They are near, I look at them
There's a white cat, once a Persian,
Now an evil zombie version
The fur upon its head has shed
Its eyes were deep and black as coal
It had no life, it had no soul
Another zombie cat was black,
It had some wounds along its back
One paw was raw, its eyes were red
It had a gash across its head,

And I could tell, that it was dead
If it could talk, it would say,
"I want to eat your brains today."
The third cat was a calico,
It seemed to me that it was slow
It had a tear across its jaw,
This zombie cat had lost a paw
The calico swayed from side to side,
As the skin peeled off its hide
They are close, I smell their reek
I lead them cross a muddy creek
The black cat slips into the muck
I am glad, as it is stuck
One cat down, two to go

Now here is a deep long pit
A rotten log lay over it
I cross and lay in wait
For they are driven by their hate
They must cross, it is their fate
Now I leap upon the log
It shakes and turns a bit,
The calico falls in the pit
The white cat crosses, fangs agleam
As John Wayne and others knew
A cat's gotta do, what a cat's gotta do
I can't go on, so I must fight,
But all it takes, is just one bite
Oh, at last, I am awake
But still I shake,
Was this all, just a dream?
I do not know, if that was so
Perhaps I am not sane
For my leg, is still in pain

TALK TO ME

Talk to me, I'll talk to you
Sometimes just a purr will do
I may howl or yowl,
But only rarely, do I growl
I give a mrow, or a meow
And sometimes I will mew for you
I purr when I am glad,
And twitch my tail when I am mad
On your lap, I will tread,
While you pet me on the head,

I'm a puss, but I'm not slow,
There are lots of words I know
Ken calls my name, I come to him,
Across the ground, I run and bound
And often good words do I hear,
"Cat treats", "Good kitty", and not least,
"Here, puss, come get your Fancy Feast."
And, "What a pretty kitty!"
"Come on my lap, and take a nap."
"Here comes Tommy, and his mommy."
Other words are not as nice
Scratch a kid and he says, "Ouch!"
Some folks yell, "Get off the couch!"
Then there are words I do not know,
"Stop it!", "Bad cat!", and "No, no, no!"

BIGGER

If I were a bit bigger,
Not a lot
I would not be an ocelot
For I have not a spot
Bobcats are big and strong
But my tail's too long
Pumas are too big and brawny,
And much too tawny
I could not be a wildcat,
Since I am a mild cat
Beneath my ears my fur is tufted.
I could be a lynx, me thinks.

KITTEN PLAY

Watch the kittens at their play
It seems like they'll play all day
One puss jumps right on her brother
Soon they are chasing one another
Oh what fun,
Three kittens in a heap
One takes a mighty leap
Look again
They're fast asleep.

"You, domestic pinky nose, come inside and warm your toes."
—HAROLD MOORE

VAMPS

It seems that vampires are all the rage,
And now are stars of screen and stage
Of handsome vamps they fantasize,
Vampy couples they romanticize
They think a ghoul is kind of cool
I disagree, I say yuck,
I think that vampires suck

At the breaking of the day,
The vampires, they go away
For in the sun, they would roast
In the sun, they would be toast
So in a darkened niche they lay
There they sleep away the day
And so their skin is pasty white
They have a nasty overbite,
And so on humans they do prey
It is a gory story
I really do not like their diet,
As a cat, I could not buy it
There exists a vampire bat,
But never, never, a vampire cat
For zombies and trolls, I have no use,
As they are into cat abuse
I think fairies are quite okay,
Meeting one would make my day
With a fairy, I would tarry
And if she shows the proper deference,
A real nice witch would be my preference.

BIG CATS

On the plain, the lions reign
A jungle's the tiger's domain
From the foliage, peers the panther
It is black with eyes of green
And the jungle is its scene
In the rainforest, lives the jaguar
Like leopards, cheetahs, and ocelots
It's a cat with lots of spots
A cougar and puma are the same,
A mountain lion by any name
These big cats are rightly feared,
As they roam in their wild home
Lions are scary, tigers are too
I'd rather be a pussycat,
And stay right here with you

ALONE TODAY

Alone today, Ken's gone away
Two days he said
The food is low,
Will I be fed?
Here comes Megan and her mommy,
And along with them is Tommy
Now I know I'll be okay
Megan puts out my food,'
Ken's daughter fills my water
I know that they will come again,
But I really miss my Ken

CALICO KITTEN

There's a kitten that I know
Suzy Q, a calico
A pussycat beauty
She's a real cutie
She looks at you
Big eyes of blue
A pretty pink pussycat nose
Tan and white are her toes
"Oh the kitty!", people gush
And turn into big piles of mush
But little kittens grow up fast
And kittenhood, it does not last
Someday Suzy, you will see
That you're a cat.
Just like me

PREY PLAY

Some folks think it's bad
Kind of sad
That cats will often play,
With their prey
Yet think of this,
While we play,
One in seven gets away.

CHEETAHS

There are cats with lots of spots,
Cheetahs, leopards, and ocelots
And way out on the African plains,
Live the lions, with big black manes
So watch out for a fast spotted cat
And if you ever meet her,
Don't play cards with her,
For she is a cheetah

HAIRBALL

On the chair, I took a nap
When I woke, I began to choke
Cough, cough, cough
I fell off
It was quick,
I am sick
I shall barf,
Right on your scarf
Okay, I'm better now
No big deal,
Just a hairball, after all

CATFISH

What's in a name?
The catfish is not a kitty
It's not even pretty
Don't count it among us friskers,
Even though it does have whiskers
The dogfish is not a dog,
It is a little shark
It does not even bark
Unlike the shark, seals do bark
We should have a dogseal, I guess
But they have whiskers, too
What a mess!

THANKSGIVING

Thanksgiving is great fun for everyone
The table is brimming,
With turkey and trimmings,
Oh my gosh, beans, yams, and squash
Everyone is eating now,
Except a hungry puss
Meow, meow, meow, meow!
Hey, hey, a kit is here,
With an empty tum,
Don't be a bum!
Give her some!
Okay, here it comes,
A real big turkey slice,
Yummy, and so very nice
Now I am sated,
And quite elated

SHADOW CAT

Shadow cat,
A tiny panther
Lurks in the garden
Waiting for the timid mouse

LITTLE BLACK CAT

Little black cat, across the street
You're a puss I'd like to meet
Why oh why, are you so shy
Come on over, look me over
I am nice, and full of spice
I'd love to play with you today
But on the grass, she does lie
She looks at me, then runs away

CAT CHRISTMAS

Christmas comes but once a year,
And when it comes, it brings good cheer,
And lots and lots of presents too
Under the tree they lie
I'll sneak a peek, as I go by
Three for me, do I see
Santa was a nice guy, then
Gee, he looks a lot like Ken
A roast beef slice, would be nice
But cook it with care, I like it rare
My wants are few
I'd like a catnip mouse or two,
And lots of love, and pets, and you

FIVE YEARS OLD

I'm five years old, and kind of bold
I have nine lives, I've used up three
I'm in good shape, or so I'm told
A pretty kitty, look at me
In the first three lives, the cat will play
In the second three, the cat will stray,
In the last three, the cat will stay
Or so they say

CAUGHT CAT

Princess and I were the good cats,
It was rare, for us to scratch a chair
But Xena was often caught,
Scratchin' where she shouldn't ought
A yell, a yowl, a water spray,
We'll see a flying cat today

"In ancient Egypt cats were worshipped as gods.
We have never forgotten."—PUSSERINA

PATCH THE PIRATE CAT

In olden times, in sunny seas
Pirates sailed the Carribees
One of these was Captain Hook
His ship was named the Booty
What he wanted, he just took
He had a wooden leg, a parrot,
And of course, a hook
He ruled the crew with an iron hand,
On the sea, and on the land
Hook was tall, lean, and mean
A vicious, fearsome, killing machine
Only one crewman was his match

A feisty one-eyed cat named Patch
On Hook's leg, the cat did scratch
Despite the Captain's roars,
The kit often sharpened his claws
Finally Hook could take no more
"At it again," the pirate roared
"Throw that dang cat overboard!"
The crew was slow to chase the cat.
Their heart was not in it
And not a one could catch,
The speedy and elusive Patch

Then the bravest of the crew
Said, "Hook, I challenge you."
Hook just laughed, and ran him through
There was no mutiny on the Booty
The angry captain said to them,
"Listen to what I say.
There's a ship in yonder bay.
First, we will go in and take her,
Then some of you will meet your maker."
The lookout cried , "A sail, a sail"
The captain jumped atop the rail
Then his wooden leg gave way
He cursed, and fell right in the bay
The crew cheered, as they sailed away

On the deck there lay,
A scratched up, splintered, piece of wood
The first mate picked it, and he did say
"Here, Patch, it's yours to scratch.
Now mateys, take a look,
At Patch, the brave little cat
Who got us off the Hook.

TOON CATS

About toon cats, I must complain
Even though, it is in vain
It's a shame, they are so lame
They give cats a real bad name
There is Sylvester and Tom too
They are losers, through and through
Jerry's a smart mouse, not a fool
He beats on Tom like a rented mule
For a mouse, he is a rat
Beating up that stupid cat
Then there is Sylvester J. Cat
As we all know, Tweety is his foe
On the net, Tweety could tweet,
"I'm a bird that can't be beat."
In fact, it could be said,
That all his wins went to his head
It's a sin, they never win
To me it is a bummer,
These two cats are dumb and dumber
As each toon ends, their fate is sealed,
They should go home and read Garfield
Or better yet, just pool their money,
And take some lessons from Bugs Bunny

CAT LOVERS OF NOTE

Many famous people loved a cat
I shall only name a few
And leave the rest to you
Let us go back in time,
and examine Egypt's sunny clime
Here, the cat they did revere,
Worshipped pusses, far and near
And when Moses set out on his quest,
He told his followers,
"Take a cat, I'll do the rest."

Some Popes, e.g., Leo VII and Pius,
Had cats who were very pious
Cat fanciers include Mohammad,
Victoria, the English queen
Actors Jimmy Stewart and Steve McQueen
Before I forget, let me say,
Cats pay homage to Doris Day
And Robert De Niro is my hero

And many writers, it is writ,
Enjoyed the company of a kit
Kipling, Wells, and E. A. Poe,
Colette and Thoreau, these I know

Emily Bronte and her sis,
Always had a cat to kiss
And then there is the great Mark Twain,
Of course, as everyone knows,
We cats simply adore his prose
Ernest Hemingway had some fifty cats,

Most of them had a pretty pink nose,
And many had some extra toes
Descendants of the cats he loved best,
Reside today, in old Key West

And several cats took up residence,
In the White House, with the Presidents
Abe, Teddy, John K., and silent Cal,
All had a kitty pal
Gerry Ford had a puss, and later on,
Cats lived there, with Bill and Ron

But legions of cat lovers remain unsung,
We have not wealth or fame,
Most people do not know our name
For that is this, and this is that,
You are the hero, to your cat

HAUNTED HOUSE

It sits alone, on a steep hill
An ancient house, it's weathered grey,
It overlooks a sheltered bay
Turrets, spires, a widow's walk
We shall visit it today
For it has an eerie history,
And contains a sense of mystery
For it is said this house is haunted
One hundred years ago
A lady lived here with her cats
And her man, who went to sea,
A captain of a ship was he
He would say, "Darling, wait for me."
And then he would go off to sea
She would don her blue shawl to watch and wait,
For she dearly loved her mate
Then one fateful day, he was lost at sea
The lady grieved, but waited there

And then, throughout the years,
The lady's cats would lick her tears
And it is said her ghost remains
You will not hear moans and chains
Instead there were sobs and cries,
Whispers and laments and sighs
Lately, those have faded away
I do not know what we will see today
Still there is a presence here,
We feel the air begin to stir
Wisps of smoke drift down the hall
The lady's ghost, in an old blue shawl

Smaller wisps follow her now,

And we hear a faint "meow"

She did not sigh, she does not cry

Instead, she smiled and passed on by

Ten steps behind her, another ghost

He wears a captain's cap, and a blue coat

It's too eerie, so we flee

And as we go, we hear him say.

"Darling wait for me"

CAT SAVES BOY: AN ODE TO TARA

Six years ago, a tabby cat, a stray
In a park alone, she did roam
Until she followed a lady home
They took her in, where she would get
A home, and, to be their pet
And later, a baby she would love
Who grew into a boy, with which to play
Sometimes, they would play all day

Now it was a sunny day,
When the boy went out to play
In the driveway on his trike
Around the car, ran the dog
He dragged the boy right off his bike
The boy yelled as his leg was bit
But soon there came a flying kit
She ran so fast, a blur of fur
Leaped and smashed the dog away
He would not bite her boy today
The dog yelped, and ran away

Tara is the pussycat's name
She cares not for wealth or fame
Tara is happy with what she gets
Love and treats and lots of pets

SALEM'S LOT

There's a new kit with my Aunt Heather
Pick him up, light as a feather
A rolly polly ball of fur
Soft and warm, and oh so new
He will give you a great big mew
Mostly black, a tad of white
Now here come the boys
They bring cat toys
Tommy, Jacob, and there's Nick
The lucky puss can have his pick
Later on, there is the girl
To watch the kitty leap and twirl
He gives a fingertip a nip
Then he licks it to be nice
Plays a bit with his toy mice
Salem is the puss's name
Being cute, is his game

CURIOSITY

Big cats are known for their ferocity,
Little ones, for their curiosity
I, for one, do poke and pry
A hole, a nook, will catch my eye
I jump into a laundry basket,
Nothing here but stinky socks,
Now I'll jump right in this box
Is there cat food in this cabinet?
Meow, meow, where's my dinner,
Look at me, I'm getting thinner
Some water in a glass, I'll taste it
Drink it up, so you won't waste it
You can look all through the house,
And never, ever, find a mouse
But then again, you never know,
Where a sneaky mouse might go
Here's a nook, I'll take a look
Don't just sit there on your fanny,
Let's go look into that cranny
They say, curiosity killed the cat,
More likely, it would kill a rat
I say, seek and you shall find
I think that it is rather odd,
That some folks sit there, like a clod
For knowledge, I have this yearning,
Just remember, life is learning

LAST POEM

And now, the last poem I have writ
I hope you enjoyed the whimsy and the wit
And the musings of this little kit
I've written in some different modes,
Limericks, sonnets, and some odes,
Lists, and quotes, and even a haiku or two
Now you may feel more affinity,
With we creatures of felinity
So goodbye my friend, we're at the end
Sad to say I go away
Perhaps we'll meet again,
Another day

THE END